Bill Milton

POETRY COLLECTION

AUSTIN MACAULEY PUBLISHERS™

LONDON • CAMBRIDGE • NEW YORK • SHARJAH

A CIP catalogue record for this title is available from the British Library.

ISBN 9781786931481 (Paperback)
ISBN 9781786931498 (Hardback)
ISBN 9781786931504 (E-Book)

www.austinmacauley.com

First Published (2018)
Austin Macauley Publishers Ltd.
25 Canada Square
Canary Wharf
London
E14 5LQ

Contents

1. The Morning Rush

Console and Berry – Morticians,
employing three dozen or more,
decided to close early one Friday,
displaying this sign on the door.

'Please ring the bell and be patient,
somebody will come down the path,
although we are shut 'til tomorrow,
we're operating a skeleton staff.'

2. Reality Shows

I had a dream that I'd become
a chicken overnight.
A Scot had worn an England shirt
and the bankers got it right.

The world's a turtle upside down,
Big Brother's off our screens.
Call centres stop at half past four
and nothing's what it seems.

Politicians always tell the truth
and most daffodils are red.
Footballers should get thousands more
for getting out of bed.

They've made me mad I told a frog,
who was playing with his vest.
A toadstool landed on his tongue
which was only done in jest.

3. Match of the Day

They came from deepest Wales and Kent,
some even drove from Reading.
From Denmark and the U.S.A.
to be at Mona's wedding.

The groom stood with his frightened look,
the best man was looking pale.
The bride walked quickly to the church,
to incarcerate her male.

'Aisle, Altar, Hymn,' she softly said –
making sure she got it right.
The organ played, the mothers cried
as the betrothed came into sight.

The vicar shouted, 'We are one down.'
The score rippled round the church.
'A choir boy has phoned in sick
and left us in the lurch.'

The groom stood at his Mona's side,
so the service could begin.
A metal object hit the grate,
the best man had dropped the ring.

With calm restored the vows were made,
the hymns were sweetly squealed.
The hatted ladies jumped with fright,
as the church bells loudly peeled.

Dozens of cameras clicked and snapped,
the photographer was stressed.
'Just look at her stood over there,
I am not at all impressed.'

(Half-Time)

Groom, bride, bridesmaid and the best man,
with the parents of the bride,
the mother and father of the groom,
friends and family to the side.

Each photo will be a treasure,
every profile will be used.
The cameras caught the flashing smiles,
but some looked quite confused.

The cars all gathered on the grid,
just like the Wacky Races.
The ushers took an early lead
to claim the hotel spaces.

The venue was a splendid sight
at the hotel 'Finally Court'.
A list pinned to the notice board,
showed what each person bought.

The best man's speech was uplifting,
even the cake was in tears.
The toast ended the proceedings,
followed by a stampede for the beers.

The couple kicked off the dancing
'Hound Dog' brought all to the floor.
The bride's dad danced like a zombie,
just like fathers had done before…

The day's highlight was the fracas,
as more guests were getting tight.
A joke aimed at Mona's uncle
ended in a drunken fight.

4. Ron Heads South

A man from the north east of England,
who played as a child by the Wear,
thought the height of sartorial fashion
was to put on his red and white gear.

One day Ron decided to travel,
where they speak with a plum in the mouth
and the geezers don't talk very clearly,
in a faraway place called the 'souff'.

Bedecked in his Sunderland colours,
he crept quietly out of the door,
with his black cat he headed for London,
like Dick Whittington did once before.

Now Ron is an honorary cockney,
who rubs shoulders with princes and queens.
Thrashing Newcastle up at St James's
is still top of his very best dreams.

Magpies don't bring very good presents,
only sorrow and sadness and mirth,
but a Mackon will always be cheerful
to death from the day of his birth.

Forget about black cats and magpies,
one memory that still brings a tear,
when Ron from the north east of England
played as a child by the Wear.

5. Rodent Kill

My hamster crashed on a roundabout
and in my head I can still hear the squeal.
I will always remember ol' Hammy
and the night that he died at the wheel.

6. Swinging Sixties

Sixty is not the end of the world,
there are still lots of things left to do.
Like telling yarns about the last war
to the young in the post office queue.

You can now buy clothes mainly for warmth
and you can pass wind without any blame,
bend the ear of that young Mister Plod,
as he helps you remember your name.

'Help the Aged' will deliver your meals
and your drugs won't cost you a cent.
You gaze at your spouse sat in his chair
and wonder 'Who is that Old Gent?'

Make sure you are helped on the bus
your fare will be paid by the State,
show the driver snaps of the grandkids
making all the other passengers late.

A retirement home needs to be picked
and it must have a bar in the loo.
No – Sixty is not the end of the world,
'cos there's still lots of things left to do.

7. Debra the Zebra

Debra the Zebra
lost one of her stripes
either a black one or white one,
there are only two types.

She wasn't aware
it had slid from her back,
until a pack of hyenas
all laughed at the crack.

8. The Man from the Pru

The insurance man knocked on the door,
'Who is it?' the parrot replied.
'It's the man from the Pru,'
said the man from the Pru,
'Will you please let me inside?'

The insurance man knocked once again,
'Who is it?' the parrot replied.
'It's the man from the Pru,'
said the man from the Pru.
'I'm looking for Christopher Hyde.'

The insurance man battered with rage,
'Who is it?' the parrot replied.
'It's the man from the Pru,'
said the man from the Pru,
then he fell on the floor where he died.

A policeman was soon on the scene.
'Who is it that recently died?'
'It's the man from the Pru,'
said the mad cockatoo.
'He was looking for Christopher Hyde.'

9. Fair-Weather Banker

The forecaster said take your umbrella,
which was foolishly left on the train
and now this very wet fella
must continue to walk in the rain.

Squelching to a bank in the City
to a huge bonus awaiting me there.
My predicament will earn me much pity
because life isn't treating me fair.

10. Spread a Little Happiness

My first is in spy, the second in tie,
the third is in Accrington Stanley.
The fourth is in puke, the next is in fluke
and the last is in weeping not manly.

The next is a cheese of distinction,
that is rarely captured in verse.
What makes this topping so different
is because it is made in reverse.

The third spread is sweet and delicious
and favoured by musicians of note,
it can be eaten when sitting in traffic
whilst wearing a really nice coat.

The fourth is a spread for the tasteless
that mum might serve with a spoon,
many people would run to avoid it,
but some would be over the moon.

The last comes from Delilah Hippa
found in a really soft state.
Work out the five that are hiding,
the minutes it takes should be eight.

(Pickle, Edam, Jam, Marmite and Philadelphia)

11. Handbags at Dawn

A crocodile swam down the Nile
underwater mile on mile.
A hunter shouted you've got style,
he raised his head and gave a smile.
Never smile if you're a crocodile.

12. Poorly Parrot

They say that a leopard keeps hold of his spots
and a rat never tells on his friend.
They say that a horse will always see sense
and a tortoise will win in the end.

They say that a crocodile will sometimes shed tears
and an elephant never forgets.
They say that an otter cannot feel cold
and tom cats have a hatred of vets.

But the one thing they never mention at all
which honestly gets on my wick,
is why does a parrot that only eats seed,
spend its life being constantly sick.

13. Eyes in the Top of My Head

Has anyone seen my specs?
I put them down for a minute or two,
where I put them I haven't a clue.
Has anyone seen my specs?

I've searched in my handbag,
I've looked in the hall.
I've checked in the bathroom
and I can not recall,
just where I left them,
off the top of my head
and just where I've been
since I got out of bed.
Has anyone seen my specs?

14. Incomplete

I hate it when things are unfinished,
I hate it when things are undone,
I hate it when things are unfinished

15. Gnome from Home

Please take pity on me,
'cos I'm gnomeless you see,
some elves killed my mum and my dad.
So I packed up my case,
washed my little round face
and stood by the road looking sad.

Then a goblin called Kev
and another named Trev
politely asked if I needed a ride.
So I climbed in their Sprite,
but things didn't go right,
they teased me so much 'til I cried.

Dumped outside the 'Red Lion' pub
in front of a slug-bitten shrub,
where people were eating their steaks.
'Can't one of you see
that this gnome refugee,
needs help 'fore his tiny heart breaks.'

Along came Minnie and Sean,
saw me looking forlorn
both invited me into the bar.
Minnie paid for a short
that's a nice touch I thought,
then a voice shouted out from afar.

'Get that gnome out of here,
He's too small to sup beer,
that beard must be stuck on with glue.
Like Will Shakespeare he's barred
with the same brush he's tarred
He must have a gnome to go to.'

'So how much would you pay
for a nice room to stay?
We think we might know of a place.'
My big ears twitched into life
for Sean and his wife,
at last put a smile on my face.

All I wanted was a gnome,
a toadstool of my own,
goldfish and a welcoming mat.
I'm moving to house number one,
where brown curtains are hung
and a rod to poke up the cat.

16. Man Flow

If you can piss you can paint,
the ceiling, the wall and the door.
It's harder to piss than to paint
without splashing the mat on the floor.

If you can paint, can you piss?
It says non-drip on the can,
make sure of your flow and don't miss
and get your aim in the pan.

17. Get Fell In

Sergeant Major Emerson Keane,
disliked Private William Green.
Bill Green knew the hatred was real
by the sergeant's command to fire at will.

18. Do We Care

Your call is important to us,
is code for we don't give a shit.
We value your custom – although
you might have to wait for a bit.

As you rage we will play you a tune,
a lesser known classical lay.
Please feel free to slam down the phone,
after one hour's continuous play.

'Hi caller, my name is Leanne,
my computer is down for a while,
I'm putting you back in the queue
– that word is offensive and vile.'

Your call is important to us,
Thanks for your patience, please hold.
Until the next operator is free,
in about half an hour we're told.

Customers are advised to take note,
the number of calls is sky high.
Gaz and Pete have gone done the pub
and Tracey is starting to cry.

Press one if you've seen a pink frog,
press two if it's started to rain,
press three for those who still want –
to stay on the line and complain.

Your call is important to us,
it is now time to end all your pain,
because everyone's going to leave.
Please ring tomorrow and start once again.

19. Why Miss

In the nineteen hundred and fifties,
we were not as bright as now.
We'd often ask the teacher why,
but never ask her how.

The moon was startled in a rhyme
by an energetic cow
and someone asked the teacher why,
but never asked her how.

20. High Five

Limericks are found at the fringe,
if you write one poets will cringe.
So never contrive,
to make the lines five
or the purists will undoubtedly whinge.

21. The One That Got Away

Jack met Gill at the ice rink,
it was their very first date.
Unfortunately, Jack pulled a muscle,
while he was learning to skate.

Perched on a bench Jack was gutted,
the poor soul looked well under par.
He'd planned to take Gill to his place,
but was unable to get in his car.

In the meantime Gill was attracted,
to a wanna-be rock star called Lee.
Who was obviously a bit of a pollock,
there are many more fish in the sea.

22. Mother's Ruin

There's something on the tele
that Granny wants tonight.
We'd better let her have it,
I think it's only right.

Ignore what's on the tele,
when Granny totters in
and takes her tumbler to the box
to fill it up with gin.

23. Don't Make Me Laugh

They say that making an audience laugh
is the hardest job you can do.
They've obviously never worked down the pit
or shovelled elephant shit in the zoo.

They say that standing alone on a stage
is the scariest place you can be.
They've never sat 'away' at the Den
or been surrounded by sharks in the sea.

They say how hard they've worked for success
and deserve their fortune and fame.
But, the thousands of carers who clean up the sick,
put their so-called work ethic to shame.

24. Take a Rest

If you really want to play snooker,
you'll have to wait for an hour or two.
Take a break in the bar with the others
and then get to the end of the queue.

25. Posh Moi

I am much posher than you,
my political colour is blue.
I eat my scones with a fork,
you scoff your scones as you talk.

I once had lunch with the mayor –
by your face you don't really care,
as you wouldn't know what to do,
that's why I am much posher than you.

I am much posher by far,
just look at my clothes and my car.
You only have grapes when you're ill,
mine are not plastic – they're real.

You call me an upper class knob,
but I'm more of a middle class snob,
Yet you answer everyone's plea
which makes you much better than me.

26. Have a Nice Day

Every dog will have its day
that is what the wise would say.
In the long grass fang will lay
for his bite of Postman Day.

27. Unfinished Sentence

The reason I escaped from my prison cell was –
I am not able to finish a sentence because –
Here is why I was caught in the very next street –
This is one sentence I will have to complete.

28. Take a Break

An old lady sat at a table,
alone on a fast moving train.
A Kit Kat lay next to her handbag
which was shabby and wet from the rain.

A man leant across to the table
and took a piece of the choccy delight,
quickly the old lady did likewise,
her whole body was shaking with fright.

Once again the man took a finger
before he got off the train.
The pensioner's face grew more angry,
but she decided not to complain.

At the next stop the lady alighted,
she desperately needed a fag,
when in shock she noticed her Kit Kat,
laying on the top of her bag.

29. Donations

The bowl marked 'For the Sick',
next to the very last pew
is just for silver and notes
and not for emergency use.

30. A Pretty Pointless Poem

Almost all alliterations are awful,
they tongue tie the teller of tales.
We worry whether words will be witty,
as first letter flow frequently fails.

31. An Injury Time Goal

I'm not a man to moan and cuss.
I never ever make a fuss,
but when you feel the way I do –
bed-ridden with this awful flu.

So in my bed I'll have to stay,
I can not go to work today.
I need my wife to be with me
to wipe my brow and bring me tea.

I do despise the whining sort,
who haven't got a caring thought,
although I'm sick and in some pain,
it's not in my nature to complain.

So from my pit I'll start to rise
and give my wife a big surprise.
I think I'm going to win my fight
and be ready for the match tonight.

32. Schooldays

I went to school and got the cane
was made to sit despite the pain,
told to play out in the pouring rain
had piles of homework once again.

'You're wrong again you sniffling rat.
Go and fetch the dunce's hat.'
Most of my schooldays were just like that,
the best days of my life.

33. The Rear Light

Billy the baboon
had red on his skin,
especially in places
where his fur was too thin.
Bill's backside was crimson
where he'd scratched at the fleas,
and the traffic all stopped
as he swung through the trees.

34. Face to Facebook

No, I'm not on bloody Facebook,
I've got better things to do,
like talking to people that I meet
to get my message through.

No – I'm not on bloody Facebook,
I would rather have a life.
I don't need to see your shopping list
or a picture of your wife.

Your weekend plans don't interest me,
I could not give a stuff.
I don't want to be among your 'pals',
one friend is quite enough.

35. Five a Day

I told you to leave the fruit alone,
the display was quite fantastic,
your turning green was no surprise,
'cos the fruit was made of plastic.

36. Words on the Street

The tables and chairs were arranged in the Crescent,
the weather was fine and the temperature pleasant.
The first to arrive was ol' Winky Pete,
in order to find the very best seat.
Following Pete were Susanna and Ed,
looking as though they came straight out of bed.
The flood gates opened as neighbours flocked out
some loaded with food and some had brought nowt.
The booze was supplied by Doctor Abe Staines
with his customary warning about hangover pains.

Soon every table was occupied in the Crescent,
some people just snarled whilst others were pleasant.
The more the drink flowed, the louder the noise,
poor Mrs Cumhardy tripped over some toys.
'Attention please,' shouted the man they all hate,
'Lift up your glasses for William and Kate'.
'I can't stand that big mouth, but his wife is quite sweet,'
said Vera Mckinley from the posh end of the street.
'Oh, no,' said big Ron as they called out some names,
'They're going to start playing ridiculous games.'

The competitive side of some in the Crescent,
saw displays of behaviour that were extremely unpleasant.
Brenda and Dave lost the three-legged race,
he was very upset by the look on his face.
He shouted the tape on his legs was tied deliberately tight.
The accusation of cheating nearly started a fight,
the day had turned sour, people drifted back home.

There was not a word spoken, just the occasional moan.
It was mid-afternoon, there was no one left in the Crescent,
the day had started quite well, but ended unpleasant.

37. A Grisly Image

I am brave and fleet of foot
and all day I've hunted bear.
Now I'm frozen half to death,
why do people stand and stare?

38. Receptionist MD

I am sorry my call was two minutes late,
the line was engaged, so I had to wait.
I know I should have rang exactly on eight
to beg for a doctor's appointment.

You've got no spare slots is that what you say?
If I need an appointment – phone on the day,
between now and then in my bed I must lay
until I get a doctor's appointment.

You require the symptoms of my complaint,
I've a pain in my neck and feeling quite faint,
up to now I have shown a lot of restraint
in seeking a doctor's appointment.

So it's your opinion that I'm not really sick,
I've acted too hasty and phoned you too quick.
You obviously think that I'm taking the mick
and you won't give me a doctor's appointment.

39. Ill Informed

I am sorry I read the last message out wrong,
sent by the daughter of Mrs O'Neil.
It shouldn't have read she's one hundred and eleven,
it should have said she was ill.

40. Let Sleeping Dogs Lie

With a pint in his hand
and a dog at his feet.
The man seemed content,
the dog looked quite sweet.

A salesman stood at the bar,
holding a lager and lime.
The pub was starting to close,
the staff had called time.

'What is this lovely mutt's name?'
'Patch' came the local's reply.
'Does your little dog bite?'
'No and neither do I.'

The man stretched out his hand
to pat the animal's head.
Blood was drawn in a flash,
turning his white cuff to red.

'You said your dog doesn't bite,
and he's not a dangerous hound.'
'My pug wouldn't hurt anyone,
he's at home safe and sound.'

41. Text Maniacs

Outside the school all the mothers are texting,
sat in a friend's house as he carried on texting.
Completely ignored it's strange and it's vexing,
wherever you go there's someone who's texting.

42. A Stone Throw Away

Let us meet at the bandstand
And should you arrive first of all.
Pick up the biggest stone you can find
And place it on top of the wall.

When I arrive at the bandstand,
The first thing that I'll do for sure,
Is pick up the stone that you left there
And throw that small rock on the floor.

43. The Winnersh Triangle

You would never believe the excuses I've heard
in order to cancel a train.
Leaves on the line, the wrong sort of snow
and even the wrong kind of rain.
The heat has buckled the rails,
the signal that fails,
a cow that won't get out of the way.
A platform's too short,
someone's stolen the salt
and frozen points that lead to delay.
The wind is blowing too strong,
the train is too long
or the driver's on strike for more pay.
The weirdest excuse which brought
a smile to my face,
was when the nine fifty vanished without any trace
and was never spotted again.

44. Optical Confusion

When I was a schoolboy of ten and a half,
I used to get plenty of sties.
An appointment was made for me to attend
to have someone examine my eyes.

I sat in a chair with a chart on the wall
when Doctor Seymour entered the room.
'I'll point to letters,' he shouted out loud,
his voice had a frightening boom

Trembling with fear and with a shake of my head
and unable to answer at all,
The largest letter at the top of the board –
was another I could not recall.

'This boy needs to be taken over the road
to see a consultant at Guys.
He can't see the letters close to his face,
so he must have bloody bad eyes.'

Each lens that was positioned invited a mist,
I wanted to get out of that place.
Lying I said the last frame was all right,
so thick glasses were made for my face.

On the way home I gripped onto the bars,
crouching down on all fours like a dog.
Slowly I moved to the edge of the kerb
and felt my way along through the fog.

A step at a time, I got nearer my home
until at last I fell through the door.
In the dimly lit hall my dad saw me sway
and was shocked by the glasses I wore.

This morning I left home seeing perfectly well,
now I'm dizzy and feeling upset.
Dad, I could not name the letters I saw
because I don't know my alphabet.

45. What Makes Granddad Grumpy

People who drop litter and think it all right,
owners of dogs who don't pick up their shite.
Drivers who park while claiming two spaces,
U.S. suspenders when in fact they mean braces.
Cats who go to toilet using my garden,
gaseous folks who never say pardon.
'Crème Anglais' on menus when it ought to say custard,
hot dogs with onions swimming in mustard.
Groups with their trolleys blocking the aisle,
bad service in shops whilst lacking a smile.
'Your call is recorded for the purpose of training',
a fine weather forecast, then it starts raining.
Politicians who say 'Let me be clear',
while telling their lies and looking sincere.
Cyclists on the road when they have their own lane,
another cancellation of my rush hour train.
Selling King Edward potatoes in kilos not pounds,
football clubs that change the name of their grounds.
Planners who want construction, but not where THEY live,
the corporations that take, but are unwilling to give.
Walkers who suddenly stop without any reason,
fish and chip platters without mushy peas on.
'Items in the bagging area when there are none'
and finally grumpy old granddads who aren't any fun.

46. Four Names

First
Prizes.
Hg
Rises

Love
Means
Blue
Jeans

Wind,
Fire,
Yellow/Green
Wire

Fourth
Sweet,
Spoils
A Treat.

47. Nightlight

When dark descends, the moths will play,
drawn to the distant light.
Why don't they come out in the day
instead of waiting until night.

48. The Ruling Class

My aunt is a lady of high standing,
is superior to the rest of us scum,
was booked into a private run clinic
to have a pimple removed from her bum.

The consultants had all been commanded
by the highest quality Harley Street men,
to administer the best sort of treatment,
so her ladyship could go home again.

Not since the bygone days of Lord Helpus
has the clinic received such a grand guest.
My great aunt, a posh lady from Ascot,
needed pampering, attention and rest.

From the doctors right up to the cleaners,
everyone made sure that they played their part.
Reacting quickly when her buzzer was buzzing
or else proceedings against them would start.

On her discharge they rolled out the red carpet
which was befitting a patient with class,
or those people in very high places
would have taken the offenders to task.

Aunt Maude went home to her grandiose mansion,
the servants guided her into a chair.
Despite trying to keep a stiff upper lip,
the pain of sitting was too much to bear.

Word soon spread about Maude's spot of bother,
her beneficiaries rushed to her bed,
some had been told the lady was poorly
while the others had heard she was dead.

49. Our Records Show

I am grateful you phoned me today
to inform me that someone must pay.
You will get me some cash
for my motor car crash,
which is not inconsequential, you say.

The accident I can not recall
as I have never driven at all,
but if you records show
that I'm entitled to dough,
send the money to Hamish McCall.

50. Fresh Kumquats Gov

Rupert Tarquin Bovington-Smythe,
always wanted to be working class.
'Why am I a merchant banker?'
a rhetorical question he asked.

Rupert Tarquin Bovington-Smythe,
dreamt of having his own market stall,
Selling watches and very old clocks.
'Caveat Emptor – Roll up one and all.'

Rupert Tarquin Bovington-Smythe,
Educated at Eton or Harrow.
You can tell he's not working class,
when he shouts, 'Get orf of one's barrow.'

51. Salt of the Earth

Sat at the funeral of Stanley McPherson,
the eulogy described this wonderful person.
There must be two Stanleys and I'm in the wrong place,
the man that I knew was a complete waste of space.

Described by the parson in the glowing of terms,
really Stan was a thug, the slimiest of worms.
He was the school bully and was rude to his mum.
Stan thought he was clever, but in fact he was dumb.

The deceased had no faults and the tributes went on,
we will miss lovely Stan, what a pity he's gone.
He gave money to tramps, helped the old cross the road,
made time for others lifting their life's weary load.

Then a list was read out which included my name,
with a sum that he left – everyone got the same.
What a generous friend, Stan was one of the best,
a true gent to the end and in peace may he rest.

52. Sailor's Knot

Charlie Jackson was a sailor,
who sailed the oceans grey.
His ship took him back to Pompey
for Charlie's wedding day.

Charles was loved by all the girls,
he had one in every port.
All his shipmates laughed out loud,
now that Charlie Boy was caught.

53. A Sonneteer Wannabe

How many lines are there in a sonnet?
To be truthful I'm not really sure.
I would so much like to pen a sonnet
like William Shakespeare did once before.
Methinks this is unlikely to happen,
I am unsure as to what I must do.
Which lines should rhyme and which ones should not,
what is the format or is there a plot?
I would cheer if I could write a sonnet
before I depart from this mortal coil.
Have I the skill I feel sure I have not?
This built-up frustration makes my blood boil,
the necessary wherewithal sadly I lack
as it appears I just don't have the knack.

54. Nag, Nag, Nag

Putting down the seat in the loo
is not so difficult to do.
Squeezing the toothpaste from the top
is something that will have to stop.
Throwing the wet towels on the floor,
hanging dirty pants on the door.
Playing darts with mates down the pub
and staying out late at the club.
Spoiling the rug with muddy shoes,
grumpy all day when your team lose.
Leaving fishing rods stood in the hall
and you never answer my call.
Keeping hold of the TV remote
and telling me which way to vote.
It's these things that upset my life;
Otherwise, you are not a bad wife.

55. What a Pantomime

Sneezy ought to blow his nose
and bashful take off all his clothes.
Dopey start to use his loaf,
Doc take the Hippocratic Oath.
Happy's smile is very cringing,
Grumpy needs to stop his whingeing
and Sleepy try to stay awake.
Snow White – get real for goodness' sake.

56. Poetic Justice

A train was at platform twenty
made up of four coaches not eight.
A message came over the tannoy,
there were five more minutes to wait.

The train for the same destination
due to leave at five fifty two
was full length with carriages empty,
except for the British Rail crew.

The first train was already heaving,
an old man was barged to the ground,
he was helped on to the next service,
where he sat alone safe and sound.

The guard waved his flag in a hurry,
the change had been missed in the din.
The commuters all stared at the old man,
who displayed his 'two-fingered' grin.

57. Lazy Days

I would like to write a book called –
'Get off your arse and get it done',
but I simply can't be bothered,
because I like sitting in the sun.

58. Don't Speak with Your Mouth Full

Sitting in the dentist's chair,
waiting for some dental care.
'Open wide you'll feel a sting,'
then he put the suction in.

'Have you been away this year?
say again I just can't hear.
Tell me if you feel some pain,
it looks like we will get more rain.'

A quick grunt was my reply,
water streaming from my eye.
Then he told a funny joke,
all this action made me choke.

59. Fish Dish

What a boney fish is skate,
salmon looks good on the plate.
Tasty cod that swims in shoals,
but the best of all are soles.

60. The Idea Shower

Today we will play 'Bullshit Bingo',
at a meeting we have to attend.
Listening out for insidious lingo,
making notes with the Corporate pen.

Parameterize and optimise,
nail the jelly to the hothouse wall.
Square the circle and incentivize,
making sure you're on the ball.

What we need is joined up thinking,
taking the helicopter's view.
Talking offline with more linking
and look under the bonnet too.

The record's on, let's see who dances,
the flag's at the top of the pole.
Who is best at seeing the chances
and taking the leadership role.

Finally the meeting's concluded.
How much bullshit did each player spot?
Who's the winner and who is deluded –
It was Len from Accounts with the lot.

61. Insensitive

I'm a very lonely hedgehog,
my friends have all been killed.
Once they started to cross the road,
their destiny was sealed.

I'm tired of the flatmate jokes,
they really make me sick.
I have overheard yet one more,
from another heartless prick.

62. A Pot to P

I took my antique to the showroom
to find what it was worth,
given to me by Uncle Sebastian
to mark the day of my birth.

What have you got? said the expert.
A Majolica pot, I replied.
Your artefact isn't Majolica,
look at the mark that's inside.

How long have you owned this ceramic
and what was the original cost?
The mark is from Torremolinos.
What your Uncle paid has been lost.

The matador that is depicted,
waving his tatty old cape,
was sold in Spain by the thousands
and the handle is held on with tape.

Because of the hole in the bottom,
you can not put anything in.
The object is totally worthless
and needs to be thrown in the bin.

63. Who's the Men in Black

Does your wife know that you're here?
Showing your white knobbly knees,
running up and down a white line
and waving a flag when you please.

Who is that man in the middle?
He is wearing identical clothes,
standing over there is another
who can't see the end of his nose.

When is matron coming for you
to take you back to your spouse?
Where you can have some hot cocoa
back at the old people's house.

64. Between Now and Next Month

I've got a leak so I've called a plumber.
He'll be here at a quarter past nine.
It's nearly twelve, no sign of the plumber,
perhaps he has got the wrong time.

I'll ring again to see what is up,
to find out why he's running late.
I'm relying on him coming today
and he hasn't muddled the date.

At last I got through to the plumber
to listen to more of his lies.
He promised he'd be with me tomorrow
as the water continues to rise.

Two days passed before he arrived
to inform me he just couldn't stop.
He was going home to write a new list
and promised I'd be at the top.

A month passed, someone else fixed the leak
and the bill was exceptionally large.
I phoned the first plumber to tell him the news
and he sent me his own call-out charge.

65. Up the Shake and Shiver

Cockney Pete didn't have the bread
to pay his Duke of Kent.
He'd Kate Moss-ed it on the horses
and his West Ham's were truly spent.

In his sky he found an Ayrton,
so he legged it down the pub
for a pint of Roger Starling
and a Harry with some grub.

Then in walked his cheese and kisses,
who marched out her heap of coke.
'Have you lost your rock of ages,
I suppose you're hearts of oak?'

A bull and cow soon erupted,
Pete would have like to Botany Bay.
He knew he was Allen Border
and his trouble would make him pay.

66. Omne Trium Perfectum

Bears furry and stout
The cheers that we shout
Three strikes and you're out

The wolf's porky feast
Wise men from the East
and a three headed beast

Blind mice like their cheese
Bad luck comes in these
Those things come in threes.

67. What's in a Name?

One of my many children
in an act that was shameless.
Never ever got christened,
so he will remain nameless.

68. Disappointment

I posted a card to my niece,
inside this message I wrote.
'Go to the shops on your birthday
and buy yourself that new coat.'

When I got back from the post-box,
there on the sideboard I spied
two fifty pound notes neatly folded,
I forgot to put them inside.

69. Unloved

People hate me because I'm a slug.
You have it easy try being a louse.
I don't feel sorry for you said the bug,
save your pity for the dirty old mouse.

The cockroach sarcastically laughed,
the rat thought it a terrible wheeze.
Why was everyone being so daft,
we should feel sorry for all the MPs.

70. L.O.

IOU46XZAJ.
IOU4ATZAB.
AGGZIOU4A
OKU3UOI-10P

71. King Lear – I Can't Hear

So young and so untender?
Sweet – No, not for me Brenda
So young, my lord, and true
Can I swap seats with you?
Let it be so! Thy truth, then be thy dower!
I just loved going to the Post Office Tower
For, by the sacred radiance of the sun,
You two have made a noise since this play begun
The mysteries of Hecat and the night;
Would the man eating crisps please be quiet?
By all the operations of the orbs
I've spilt my coke – I hope this tissue absorbs!
From whom we do exist and cease to be;
If you are buying popcorn get some for me
Here I disclaim all my parental care,
Would you stop kicking the back of my chair?
Propinquity and property of blood,
Brenda, can I have a swig of your Bud?
And as a stranger to my heart and me
Would you please sit down so that I can see?
Hold thee from this for ever
Flicking peanuts is not very clever.

72. Shell Shocked

Granny's got a winkle pin,
she kept it in a special tin.
Silently a thief crept in –
she hasn't got a winkle pin.

Granny grabbed her rolling pin
and chased the felon who broke in.
The neighbour heard an awful din,
now Granny's got her winkle pin.

73. Sammy the Shark

Sammy the Shark is a very young fish,
he smiles when he glides, his tail gives a swish.
Sammy the Shark could not understand
when he swims in the bay people stay on the land.

74. Rough Justice

Mister McBane gave me the cane
because I didn't listen at school.
Six of the best for failing a test
which to me seemed a little bit cruel.

Mister McBane can't give the cane
because they've changed all of the rules.
This teacher is sad, the pupils are glad
which makes for far happier schools.

Mister McBane has broken his cane
and thrown the two halves in the bin.
Now his own cane gives him much pain
because a splinter shot under his skin.

75. Eagle Eyes

A drone flew over Islington,
way up in the north London sky.
A bird of prey had spotted it,
downing the machine from on high.

The eagle was in the police force,
one of many ambitious young plod.
This act might earn him promotion
to a place on the Special Branch squad.

76. Persecuted

Why do the non-smokers keep bitching,
because I light up in their kitchen.
Every time I smoke at the store,
I am quickly shown to the door.
When outside a restaurant I stand,
someone will still flap their hand.
My friend is Fire and I'm called Smoke,
nicknames to make us the butt of the joke.
So you non-smokers please give us a break,
we'll smoke our fags and you eat your cake.

77. Behaving Like Animals

Five creatures went to a party,
where they consumed loads of booze.
The bird was dressed really tarty,
in feathers and glitzy red shoes.

The tick was as tight as elastic,
The fish was still drinking at nine.
The newt felt really fantastic
and the kite was high on white wine.

The giraffe banged on the ceiling,
the noise was hard to believe.
Everyone left – some were reeling,
the skunk was the last one to leave.

78. In a Puff of Smoke

It was what my dear mum always feared,
when the smoke in the room slowly cleared,
as I stood in my cloak and long beard,
I was looking decidedly weird.
My family and friends loudly cheered,
when my conjurers set disappeared.

79. A.W.O.L.

Bob Blair was an excellent boss,
admired by all of his staff.
Bob was the most forward thinker
at Robertson, Jones and McGrath.

The oldest man in his section
was Leonard Barrington-Sears.
Who was married to Lolita-Consuela,
they'd been together for thirty four years.

One Monday morning in April,
Leonard failed to turn up for work.
He sometimes took the odd sick day,
he could be a man who would shirk.

In order to check all was well,
a phone call was made to Len's house.
A good neighbour softly reported
that Leonard had lost his dear spouse.

Tell Len his colleagues are sorry,
devastated at his sad loss.
He mustn't come back 'til he's ready
and we will inform Leonard's boss.

A week had passed without contact,
Robert Blair was asked to find out,
if Barrington-Sears was still coping
and should he need help he must shout.

When Robert Blair walked to the door,
he got the surprise of his life,
the person stood on the front step
was Leonard's much grieved over wife.

I'm sorry Mrs Barrington-Sears
we assumed you had passed away.
We haven't heard from your husband
not since that unfortunate day.

I don't understand what you're saying,
I went to the shops and got lost.
My husband found me outside Sainsbury's
at the point where the shopping malls cross.

Thank you for showing such kindness
and for giving us time to recover.
Len's at the lake 'til this evening,
fishing for trout with his brother.

80. Oh for the Days of the Threepenny Bit

Granddad's room sizes written on card
are seldom by metre mostly by yard.
Baby's weight is recorded by pound,
it's much better than kilos would sound.

Our eggs are sold in dozens not tens,
laid in Britain by imperial hens.
Beer is in pints and petrol in litres,
horses run furlongs, athletes run metres.

Mum weighs her sugar when making jams,
she measures in ounces never in grams.
Father likes his jam spread on his scones,
in the last month he's put on two stones.

Someone resolved twelve months is a year.
Why there is not ten is very unclear.
There are twelve hours on a clock face,
A ten hour dial looks out of place.

Oh for the days of the threepenny bit,
wool bought in ounces ready to knit.
Give them an inch, they'll take your mile,
many a mickle will make us all smile.

81. Pride Comes Before a Fall

Ripley the lion stared out of his cage,
he was put behind bars at a very young age.
He hated the people who mimicked his roar
or the ones who pretended to open his door.
A man smartly dressed had a very close shave,
he pulled Ripley's tail to show he was brave.
When the lion kept still he started to brag,
pretending to bum him with the end of his fag.
The moron turned to the crowd fisting the air
'I am the type that a lion can't scare.'
The man made a mistake by turning away,
Ripley suddenly sprang from the place where he lay.
Losing some weight and his insidious grin,
his legs turned to jelly as the claws ripped his skin.
The magnificent beast stood looking proud
and I'm sure I noticed him wink at the crowd.

82. A Working Dog

My dog is called Blacksmith,
why it is I'm not sure.
When I rattle his lead
he makes a bolt for the door.

83. All Is Lost

I have lost my hair
I've lost my teeth
I'm an unbearable consumer.
I've lost my memory
I've lost my memory
and I've lost my sense of humour.

84. Help Out the Heroes

A council director named Wiggins
thought he was cock of the walk.
He spoke at all of the meetings
and oh how Wiggy could talk.
'I've got an idea,' said Lou Wiggins,
'To make the Council some dough –
charge yearly for memorial panels
or out of the Chapel they'll go'.
The chamber went eerily silent
until Kirsty Annabel White
said, 'Some plaques belong to our heroes
and to discard them just wouldn't be right.'
The objection was quietly glossed over
and the motion went through very quick.
This cynical fund raising venture
made the decent people feel sick.
The invoices were soon in the post,
reaching homes the very next day.
Many had changed their address
and some were unable to pay.
After twelve months had elapsed,
the money had failed to arrive
with this one despicable act
reputations just could not survive.
In the Chapel results could be seen
like Rupert the walls were all bare,
Councillor Lou Wiggins Deceased
was the only memorial there.

85. Me and Bertie Cottle

Me and Bertie Cottle
went to White Hart Lane,
Bertie threw a stink bomb
so we never went again.
On our way to Camden
we shared a bag of chips
plus half a can of cola
taking alternating sips.

Me and Bertie Cottle
did a paper round.
Bertie switched the 'Tit-Bits'
with the 'Horse and Hound'.
The colonel got the 'Tit-Bits'
which made his vision blurred,
the vicar was quite angry,
but never said word.

Me and Bertie Cottle
went along to see
a legend rock and roller
by the name of Jerry Lee.
Jerry Lee was shaking,
so were Bert and me,
both very smug and happy
because we'd sneaked in free.

Me and Bertie Cottle
biked to Regents Park,
the time passed by so quickly,
we were there 'til after dark.
That was the last time I saw Bertie
as I went my separate way,
it's been over sixty years,
but I'm seeing him today.

86. When Your Number Is Up

An old lady went to the deli
for salami, tongue and some brie,
she tore off the next ticket showing
which was number one hundred and three.
Then she had a senior moment
and thought she'd tear off some more,
ripped off a new batch of numbers
that went up to two hundred and four.
The old dear moved from the counter
throwing the strip of paper away,
then along came another old biddy
and took the next one on display.
After twenty minutes of waiting
her number still failed to show,
Her frustration soon turned to anger
as the queue continued to grow.
The old lady grew tired and weary
and became giddy and needed a stool,
the tannoy called Phyllis from Produce,
who made an emergency call.
The paramedics arrived very quickly
and carried her out of the store,
her number was called as she left –
'Where was two hundred and four'?

87. Tom, Dick or Harry

From the end of the pier,
looking out at the sea,
stood Richard, Harold, Thomas and me.
Which of us would speak first,
which one would it be –
Richard, Thomas, Harold or me?
Which one was the culprit?
It could not have been me.
Would Richard, Thomas or Harold agree?
I was not even there,
I was drinking with Lee –
We never got home 'til twenty past three.
The vicar was angry,
when at last he could see,
his favourite wig had been nailed to a tree.
It might have been Tom.
It could have been Dick.
Perhaps even Harry – any one of the three!

88. It's One of Those

There was a creature that lived in my house,
it hung out under the sink.
Its arms were blue and its legs were all green,
the rest of its body was pink.
This strange thing was the size of a nut
and turned itself inside out.
When it got into that strange position,
all that was seen was a snout.
The sound that it made was unusual
like a coin scratching on tin.
It ran pass me and into the garden
and I never saw it again.
I wonder what happen to walnut
and why he left me that day,
perhaps it's under the sink in your house,
make sure you don't scare it away.

89. Green with Envy

I need my four by four to take the boys to school,
the car park is uneven and the weeds are very tall.
If an elephant should charge or a tank get in my way,
my kids will be safe inside and will see another day.

I need my four by four so to Waitrose I can pop,
I really want two spaces when I do my weekly shop.
I must be up high and look down on smaller cars,
They will all envy me with my shining cattle bars.

I need my four by four to speed along the road,
making sure that all the others obey the Highway Code.
After such a heavy day I drive up to my bank
to draw out loads of money so I can fill the tank.

90. Not Another Superhero

I am a superhero
righting every wrong.
My name is Mister Sarcastic
and Mummy says I'm strong.
My sidekick is Ironic Boy,
who wears an orange cape.
He can be found at 'Muscles Gym'
that's where he keeps in shape.
We put more cones on England's roads
to help with traffic flows.
We will use our special powers
to make more food-based shows.
The fat cats are our latest cause
and when they don't succeed.
they lose some of their bonus cash
with hungry mouths to feed.
One day we will star in a film –
called 'The Sarcastic Two'.
A tale about the oppressed rich
and the selfless work they do.

91. Mononymous

Adele, Cher and Lucy
Eric, Erne and Brucie.
Peter, Paul and Mary
Sporty, Baby, Scary.
Ginger, Posh and Dolly
Buster, Stan and Ollie.
Chas and Dave, Ant and Dec
Gazza, Pele, Saint and Becks.
Satchmo, who could sing low
Paul, John, George and Ringo.
Kermit and Miss Piggy,
Madonna, Oprah, Twiggy.
Cilla, Tarby, Yoko
Pete and Dud and Coco.
Stalin, Franco, Monty
Beefy, Freddie, Jonty.
Harpo, Chico, Groucho
Socrates and Plato.
Zsa Zsa and Sabrina
Singers Ike and Tina.
Bonnie, Clyde and Blackbeard
outlaws that they all feared.
Napoleon and Scarface
sent off to a far place.
Elvis, Prince, Seal and Bing
Bono, Suggs, Meatloaf, Sting.
Lulu, Britney, Kylie
Rihanna, Sade and Miley.
Will. I. am and Bowie

Banksy, Einstein, Lowry.
All above have found fame
each is known by one name.

92. Rain Stopped Play

Teachers and parents all huddled together,
nobody predicted the change in the weather.
The field was a quagmire, kids soaked to the skin,
the man in the middle said the match must begin.
The first shot of the day caught the keeper off guard,
the ball slipped through his hands hitting him hard.
A man in the crowd shouted, 'Get to your feet,'
the Headmaster liked all his boys to compete.
The boy's Dad shouted back, 'You're a disgrace –
How would you like a smack in the face?'
The Headmaster shouted, 'Enough is Enough –
Boys at my school really need to be tough.'
He left shortly after shaking his head,
nobody could believe what he had said.
The new keeper was on the field of play
and he threw the ball a very long way.
The first boy gave chase, the next said, 'It's mine,'
the third man stopped it from crossing the line.
Then suddenly the heavens opened again,
everyone ran to get out of the rain.
The torrential storm decided to yield
within a few minutes both sides took the field.
One of the two strikers hit the ball high,
everyone watched as it fell from the sky.
The ball landed and stuck in a mud patch
which turned out to be the end of the match.
No one was left to huddle together,
the game was spoilt by the terrible weather.

The crowd didn't see the fall of a wicket,
it was not the right day for the boys to play cricket.

93. Wexit

We've written to the Government
as I think you knew we might,
to demand a referendum
for an independent Isle of Wight.
If it's good enough for Scotland,
it is good enough for us,
to seek self determination
with the minimum of fuss.
We will adopt the Shanklin shilling
with a parliament in Ryde
from the Needles east to Bembridge,
you should back the 'Yes' vote side.

Barney May from Sandown
will lead the vote to remain,
John Johnson, out of Newport
will head the Leave campaign.
We must limit immigration
plus what comes out of Cowes,
and for no rhyme or reason
we will only trade with Wales.
No one will write on buses
residents must have their say.
those Islanders who wish to leave
will all be forced to stay.

94. Some You Win and Some You Lose

Should I buy a lottery ticket
and which numbers should I choose?
I'll purchase one at random
from a shop I always use.
Wednesday came I fetched a pen
from my lucky tin.
I sat and waited with Patience
and wondered if I'd win.
The first one out was thirty two,
then twenty four and seven,
three, six and forty one
and the bonus ball eleven.
I wrote the numbers in a line
and placed the paper on a stool.
It was time for Patience's daily walk,
she was waiting in the hall.
While I was out my wife returned
with her sisters Pam and Nelly
she saw the numbers laying there
and checked them with the tele.
When I got home the ladies slept,
Champagne bottles strewn on the floor.
God help me when the morning comes
and I tell them we're still poor.

95. Cock-a-Snook

Robin was dating a Wren name of Mary,
they met at a club called 'The Singing Canary'.
Mary's betrothed needed eyes like a hawk,
his rival was Al who was cock of the walk.
The love birds went to the pub for a bite,
Rob's opponent was there as high as a kite.
They ordered a Grouse and half pint of Hen
amid foul expletives from some of the men.
The larking about went over the top,
the pair turned around and asked them to stop.
Huffing and puffing Al swallowed his beer,
he stood and staggered and fell on his rear.
Perched on his stool was big Dickie Macrow,
who told the love birds they really should go.
The couple agreed it was time to take flight
'cos some of the men were wanting to fight.
They had to duck as they made their way out
because someone had thrown a bottle of stout.
The sound of the sirens could not be heard,
so Al and his mates all had to do bird.

96. A Change Is as Good as a Rest (Unless You're a Snooker Player)

I get up every night to go for a pee
sometimes it's twice, more often it's three,
when I return to continue my sleep –
the sheets have been changed, the old in a heap.
Awoken at dawn by two crowing cocks,
searching around for my dirty old socks.
'They're in the wash along with your pants –
change them more often,' the good lady rants.
'You need to change if we're to agree.'
The final warning my spouse gave to me.
There was a time when I saw lots of change,
ten bob from a pound really wasn't that strange.
At last I took heed of what I was told
and altered my ways before I grew old.
Finally, I made a change to my life –
I managed to find a much younger wife.

97. Nostalgia Is Not
What It Used to Be

Remember the days of the black and white tele,
dripping in bread and eels floating in jelly.
Mums wearing pinnis with a scarf on their head
councils that listened to what people said.
Coppers that washed and mangles that squeezed,
the foreman who did whatever he pleased.
Footballers turned out for a couple of bob,
if they could get time off from their job.
Telephone boxes where there used to be queues,
no trainers existed only well polished shoes.
Policeman that gave you the time of the day,
avoiding the rent man when you couldn't pay.
Political correctness had yet to arrive,
common sense was used in a bid to survive.
Archie and Peter could be heard on the 'Light'
Peter, the vent, must have kept his mouth tight.
The nit nurse came to the school every week,
Vincent Price at the flicks made us all freak.
Searching the bombsites for what we could find,
when the Queen Mother came the streets were all lined.
The man from the Pru called each Friday night,
a gas lamp gave us a glimmer of light.
The rich had their own TV to view
and we went outside to go to the loo.
A spoon full of malt was forced down our throats,
only the posh kids had button-up coats.
A best room was kept in case somebody called
nobody came – we were easily fooled.

The coal was delivered by horse and cart,
beans covered in salt were good for our heart.
Round baths and pig bins made out of metal,
the sound of a whistle that came from the kettle.
Dinner was at noon and tea was at four,
we never needed to deadlock the door.
We kept in touch using paper and pen,
nostalgia's not what it used to be then.

98. Random Thoughts

Start the day happy
Muesli makes U smile.
Storage of data –
A life in a file.
Crumbs from a sandwich –
Food found in a beard.
Electrical faults –
Wired wrongly is weird.
Des comes from Leeds, but –
Tina is from Staines.
Bess is found in buses
and Ian seen in trains.
Kay's sat in the front
Her craft goes both ways –
The river is calm –
her canoe gently sways.
Can't make the Wall Game
Sent note back to school.
Dived in the water –
Loop back out the pool.
Calories counted –
Two weight-watchers tied.
Both seem quite happy –
With the diet they tried.

99. A Case of Mistaken Identity

The five twenty two through the countryside sped.
A large suitcase sat in the rack overhead.
Nobody spoke, not a single word said.
Newspapers crumbled with many unread.

The first station was reached, a passenger slept.
He was jolted awake and through the door leapt.
Another commuter his wits he had kept.
Grabbed the suitcase and threw it onto the wet.

A fellow traveller stood up and he cried.
'Why is my luggage on the platform outside?'
The other people had their mouths open wide.
One of the group wished he'd curled up and died.

100. What's Your Problem?

Just because you bully me,
doesn't make you strong.
Just because I'm different,
doesn't make me wrong.
Just because you think you're liked,
doesn't mean you are.
Just so you can have your fun,
I must bear the scar.
Just because I get upset,
doesn't mean I'll fold.
You will pay the price one day,
when you're lonely, sad and old.